# Michele Bachmann: A to Z

Ron Paul Jones

The image on the front cover derive from

Michele Bachmann's official U.S. government photo.

# Contents

# Contents

# A

## Attention

Michele Bachmann can draw attention wherever she goes. She appears on cable news shows, at rallies, and other gatherings. She is attractive and articulate. Whether people love her or hate her, they pay attention to her.

# B

## Bailout

Michele Bachmann voted against both versions of the Bailout of the U.S. Financial System. This won her a lot of support and respect from Tea Party members.

# C

## Christian

Michele Bachmann is an evangelical Christian. She attends a Christian non-denominational church. She is pro-Life.

# D

## Driven

Michele Bachmann is driven for political success. She started off small, first at the local level. She later rose to the state level, and then to the national level. She has the drive needed to become President of the United States.

# E

## Enthusiasm

Michele Bachmann has enthusiastic supporters. They contribute money and manpower to her campaign. She has a very formidable organization.

# F

## Financial Superstar

Michele Bachmann is a financial superstar. Her fundraising numbers are mind-boggling. She was able to raise over $13 million to defend her House seat.

# G

## Grassroots Support

Michele Bachmann has significant grassroots support. Much of her fundraising money was small contributions from individuals.

# H

## Huckabee

Michele Bachmann has Mike Huckabee to thank. Because Huckabee decided not to run for President, Bachmann was able to gain many of his supporters. Huckabee's decision also opened up the Iowa caucus, as well as Southern and Midwestern primaries.

# I

## Intelligence Committee

Michele Bachmann serves on the House Permanent Select Committee on Intelligence. This gives her the intelligence and national security credentials that are helpful for a Presidential run.

# J

## Jimmy Carter

Michele Bachmann supported Jimmy Carter in 1976. She and her husband even worked on Jimmy Carter's campaign for President.

# K

## K-12 Charter School

In 1993, Michele Bachmann helped start a K-12 charter school in Stillwater, Minnesota.

# L

## The Letter "L"

Michele Bachmann's first name contains only one "L". No doubt many people will misspell her name. Remember that the correct spelling of her first name is "Michele"

# M

## Mother

Michele Bachmann is the mother of five children. Her children are Lucas, Harrison, Elisa, Caroline, and Sophia.

# N

## National Figure

Despite being a Congresswoman, Michele Bachmann has become a national figure. She raised her national profile by becoming a key leader of the Tea Party movement.

# O

## Outspoken

Michele Bachmann is known for being very outspoken. She has been a frequent critic of Democrats and President Obama.

# P

## Populist

Michele Bachmann has populist credibility.  She does not have an elitist background and did not graduate from Ivy League schools.  She can communicate and relate with Middle America.

# Q

## Quotes

Michele Bachmann often gets ridiculed for her quotes.  But she keeps on talking for the news media.  Perhaps Bachmann understands that any publicity is good publicity.

# R

## Representative

Michele Bachmann is a member of the U.S. House of Representatives. She represents Minnesota's 6th Congressional District. She could become the first sitting Representative to win the Presidency in over 100 years.

# S

## State of the Union Response

Michele Bachmann gave the Tea Party response to President Obama's 2011 State of the Union address. She stole a lot of thunder from Paul Ryan, who gave the official GOP response. Bachmann's nationally broadcast response further raised her national profile.

# T

## Tea Party

Michele Bachmann is a leader of the Tea Party movement. She became prominent in the Tea Party by being a very outspoken opponent of President Obama. She founded the House Tea Party Caucus in July 2010.

# U

## Underdog

Michele Bachmann started her campaign for President as an underdog. Many people wrote her off and underestimated her. She appears to perform well in the role of underdog.

# V

## Victorious

Michele Bachmann has been victorious in every state and national election in which she has competed. She has won seats in the Minnesota Senate and U.S. House of Representatives. Her next target is the White House.

# W

## Waterloo, Iowa

Michele Bachmann was born in Waterloo, Iowa on April 6, 1956. Bachmann announced her candidacy for President of the United States in Waterloo. This was a masterful decision because it allowed her to reconnect with her roots, while connecting with Middle America.

# X

## E<u>x</u>citing

Michele Bachmann is an exciting candidate.  When she talks, people pay attention.  She has a very strong and loyal group of supporters.

# Y

## Youth Vote

Michele Bachmann will challenge Ron Paul for the youth vote in the GOP primaries. If successful, she will try to seize a chunk of the youth vote from President Obama.

# Z

## Zealous

Michele Bachmann's supporters are a zealous group. They love her, they love her, they love her.